# Fast Fat-Quarter
## QUILTS

Martingale®
*Create with Confidence*

Fast Fat-Quarter Quilts

© 2013 by Martingale & Company®

**Martingale**

19021 120th Ave. NE, Ste. 102
Bothell, WA 98011-9511 USA
ShopMartingale.com

Printed in the United States of America
18 17 16 15 14 13      8 7 6 5 4 3 2 1

**Library of Congress Cataloging-in-Publication Data is available upon request.**
ISBN: 978-1-60468-345-5

Mission Statement
Dedicated to providing quality products
and service to inspire creativity.

# Contents

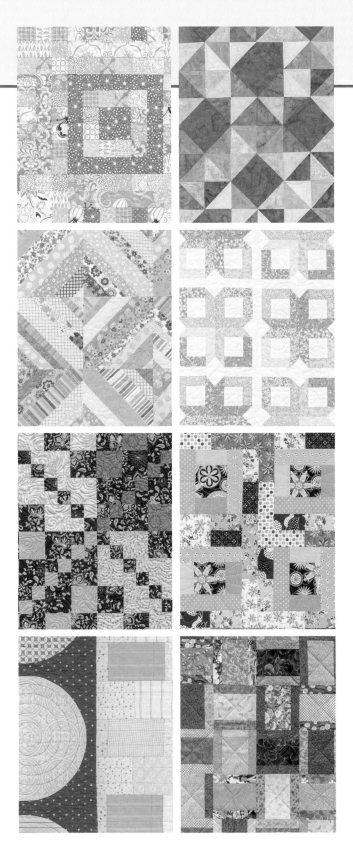

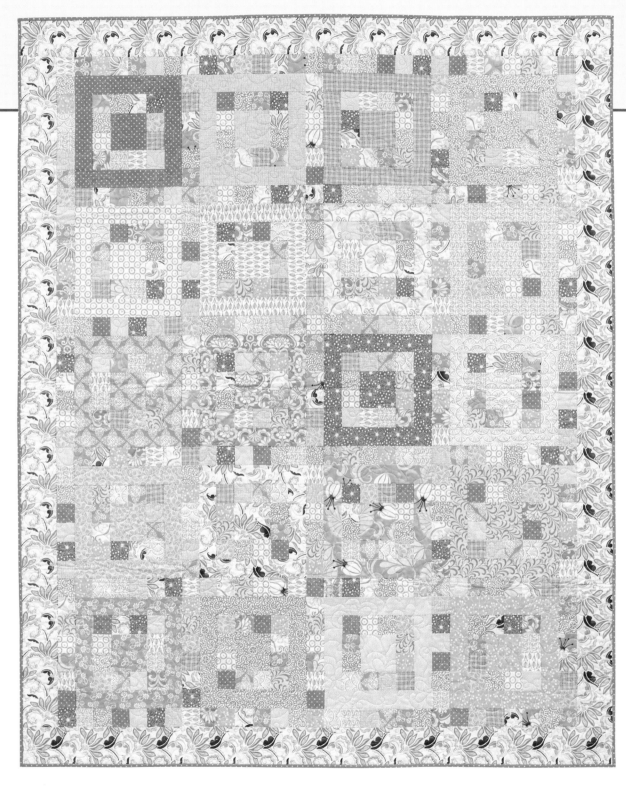

Designed and pieced by Tracy Overturf; machine quilted by Lynn Reppas

**Quilt size:** 66½" x 80½" • **Block size:** 12" x 12"

# Sherbet Punch

*Collecting the fat quarters for this quilt is half the fun. Just pick a color scheme and look for those colors at each quilt shop you visit. When you look at the finished quilt, you'll have fun memories.*

## Materials

*Yardage is based on 42"-wide fabric; fat quarters are 18" x 21".*

20 assorted fat quarters for blocks and sashing*
1⅛ yards of fabric for border
⅔ yard of fabric for binding
5 yards of fabric for backing
73" x 87" piece of batting

*\*Don't prewash the fabrics in this case; you'll need the full size of the unwashed fat quarters to cut the pieces needed.*

## Cutting

*All measurements include ¼"-wide seam allowances.*

### From *each* fat quarter, cut:
1 strip, 5" x 21"; from each strip, cut 1 square,
   4½" x 4½" (20 total). Cut the remainder of the strip
   lengthwise into 2 strips, 2½" wide. From each strip
   cut 1 rectangle, 2½" x 12½" (40 total), and 1 square,
   2½" x 2½" (40 total).
1 strip, 2½" x 21"; crosscut into 2 rectangles,
   2½" x 8½" (40 total), and 1 square, 2½" x 2½"
   (20 total)
4 strips, 2½" x 21" (80 total; 4 will be extra)

### From the border fabric, cut:
8 strips, 4½" x 42"

### From the binding fabric, cut:
8 strips, 2½" x 42"

## Making the Blocks

1 Sew two assorted 2½" x 21" strips together to make a strip set; repeat to make a total of 10 strip sets. Press the seam allowances toward the darker fabric in each set. Cut each strip set into eight units, 2½" x 4½", for a total of 80 units.

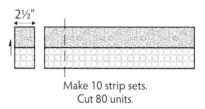

Make 10 strip sets.
Cut 80 units.

2 Sew units from step 1 to opposite sides of a 4½" square, making sure to use different-colored units. Press the seam allowances toward the center square. Make 20.

Make 20.

3 From the remaining 2½" x 21" strips, create five groups of four strips each, making sure to use four different fabrics in each set. Sew the strips in each set together and press the outer seam allowances outward and the inner seam allowances in either direction. Cut each strip set into eight units, 2½" x 8½", for a total of 40 units.

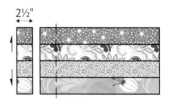

Make 5 strip sets.
Cut 40 units.

4 Sew units from step 3 to the remaining sides of each unit from step 2, making sure to vary the fabrics. Press the seam allowances toward the top and bottom units.

5 Sew 2½" x 8½" rectangles that match the center square to opposite sides of each block. Press the seam allowances toward the rectangles. Sew matching 2½" x 12½" rectangles to the top and bottom of each block. Press the seam allowances toward the rectangles. The blocks should measure 12½" x 12½".

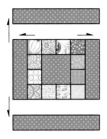

Make 20.

6 For the sashing, make six strip sets of six assorted 2½" x 21" strips each. Cut each strip set into eight units, 2½" x 12½", for a total of 48 units. Press the seam allowances on each end inward and the remaining seam allowances in either direction.

2½"

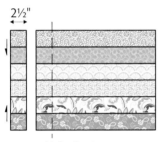

Make 6 strip sets.
Cut 48 units.

## Assembling the Quilt Top

1 Arrange the blocks and sashing strips into a horizontal row as shown. Sew one sashing strip to the left side of each block and to the left and right sides of the last block in the row. Press the seam allowances toward the blocks. Sew the blocks and their sashing strips together. Press the seam allowances toward the blocks. Make five rows.

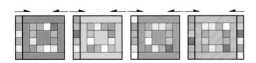

Make 5.

2 Randomly sew leftover strip sets of six and two squares, along with single squares, into six sashing strips of 29 pieces each.

Make 6.

3 Sew the sashing strips to the top of each row and to the top and bottom of the last row. Join the rows. Press the seam allowances toward the block rows.

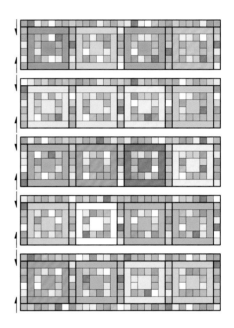

4 Sew two border 4½" x 42" strips together; repeat to make four long strips. From those strips, cut two 72½"-long strips and sew them to the sides of the quilt top. Press the seam allowances toward the borders.

5 Cut two 66½"-long strips and sew them to the top and bottom of the quilt top. Press the seam allowances toward the borders.

## Finishing the Quilt

Go to ShopMartingale.com/HowtoQuilt for free downloadable information on finishing your quilt.

1 Piece and trim the backing to measure approximately 6" larger than the quilt top.

2 Layer the backing, batting, and quilt top; baste. Quilt as desired.

3 Trim the excess batting and backing even with the quilt top.

4 Use the 2½"-wide strips of binding fabric to make and attach double-fold binding.

# Ocean Waves

*Hourglass blocks are very easy to make, and if you stack your fat quarters and cut all the pieces at once, you'll save loads of time, too. In the end, you'll have a dynamic-looking quilt with lots of movement!*

## Materials

*Yardage is based on 42"-wide fabric; fat quarters are 18" x 21".*

10 fat quarters of assorted batik solids for blocks
1⅓ yards of solid blue batik for blocks and borders
½ yard of fabric for binding
3½ yards of fabric for backing
63" x 63" piece of batting

## Cutting

*All measurements include ¼"-wide seam allowances.*

**From the solid blue batik, cut:**
8 strips, 5¼" x 42"; crosscut into:
    4 strips, 5¼" x 38¼"
    24 squares, 5¼" x 5¼"

**From *each* of the 10 fat quarters, cut:**
8 squares, 6" x 6"; cut into quarters diagonally to yield
    320 triangles (28 will be extra)
3 squares, 4¼" x 4¼"; cut in half diagonally to yield 60
    triangles (8 will be extra)

**From the binding fabric, cut:**
7 strips, 2¼" x 42"

## Making the Blocks

1 Randomly select and sew together two 6" triangles along the short edges as shown. Repeat to make a total of 146 triangle units. Do not press the seam allowances yet.

Make 146.

2 Randomly select two triangle units from step 1. Press the seam allowance of one unit in one direction and the seam allowance of the other unit in the opposite direction. Sew the units together to complete the Hourglass block. Repeat to make a total of 73 blocks.

Make 73.

## Assembling the Quilt Top

1 Randomly sew together two 4¼" triangles along the short edges as shown. Repeat to make a total of 24 pieced side setting triangles. The remaining four triangles are the corner triangles.

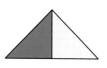

Make 24.

2 Set aside 12 Hourglass blocks for the border. Refer to the quilt assembly diagram on page 9 to arrange the remaining blocks, the blue batik 5¼" squares, and the side setting triangles into diagonal rows. Sew the pieces in each row together. Press the seam allowances in opposite directions from row to row.

3 Sew the rows together. Press the seam allowances away from the center row. Add the corner triangles last. Press the seam allowances toward the triangles.

Designed and pieced by Terry Martin; machine quilted by Adrienne Reynolds

**Quilt size:** 56¾" x 56¾"  •  **Block size:** 4¾" x 4¾"

**4** Sew Hourglass blocks to both ends of each blue batik 5¼" x 38¼" strip. Press the seam allowances toward the strip. Sew two of these strips to the sides of the quilt top. Press the seam allowances toward the border. Add two more Hourglass blocks to each end of the remaining two strips. Sew these strips to the top and bottom of the quilt top. Press the seam allowances toward the border.

## Finishing the Quilt

Go to ShopMartingale.com/HowtoQuilt for free downloadable information on finishing your quilt.

**1** Piece and trim the backing to measure approximately 6" larger than the quilt top.

**2** Layer the backing, batting, and quilt top; baste. Quilt as desired.

**3** Trim the excess batting and backing even with the quilt top.

**4** Use the 2¼"-wide strips to make and attach double-fold binding.

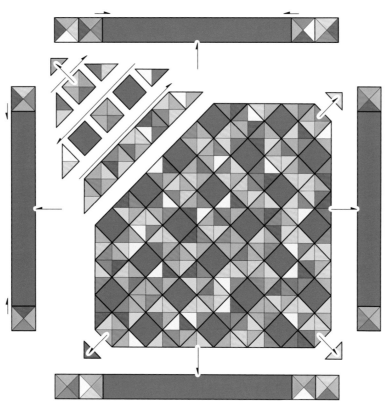

Quilt assembly

Designed and pieced by Mary Jacobson and Barbara Groves

**Quilt size:** 71" x 75" • **Block size:** 10" x 10"

# String Beans

*Calling all colors! Collect "string beans," or strips, from your favorite fabrics to create this cheerful cuddle-up quilt. Sewing string beans onto a foundation square will keep your bias under control.*

## Materials

*Yardage is based on 42"-wide fabric; fat quarters are 18" x 21".*

36 assorted fat quarters for blocks
4 yards of white muslin for block foundations
⅝ yard of pink print for border
⅝ yard of green print for border
½ yard of yellow print for border
½ yard of orange print for border
¾ yard of striped fabric for binding
5 yards of fabric for backing
79" x 83" piece of batting

## Cutting

*All measurements include ¼"-wide seam allowances.*

**From *each* fat quarter, cut:**
2 strips, 2¾" x 21" (72 total)
2 strips, 2¼" x 21" (72 total)
2 strips, 1¾" x 21" (72 total)
2 strips, 1¼" x 21" (72 total)

**From the muslin, cut:**
12 strips, 11" x 42"; crosscut into 36 squares, 11" x 11"

**From *each* of the yellow and orange prints, cut:**
2 strips, 5¾" x 42" (4 total)

**From *each* of the pink and green prints, cut:**
2 strips, 7¾" x 42" (4 total)

**From the striped fabric, cut:**
8 strips, 2¼" x 42"

## Making the Blocks

1 Place a fat-quarter strip of any width *right side up* diagonally across the center of an 11" muslin foundation square.

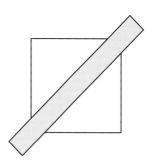

2 With right sides together, place another fat-quarter strip on top of the center strip; align the side edges. Make sure your strips always extend beyond the muslin foundation.

3 Stitch a ¼" seam along the edge through all layers. Flip and press toward the corner.

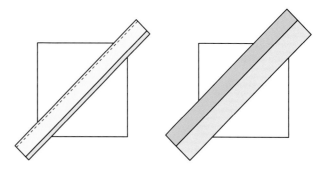

4 Continue adding strips to each side of the center strip until the muslin foundation is completely covered. Be creative; use different widths and colors so that no two blocks are the same.

5 From the back side, trim the blocks (including both the muslin foundation and the top fabrics) to measure 10½" square. The muslin foundation helps control the bias edges of the strips. The trimmed-off pieces can be used in other projects. Repeat all steps to make 36 blocks.

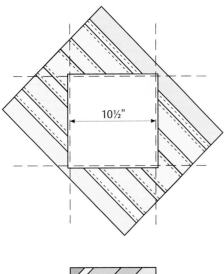

Make 36.

## Assembling the Quilt Top

1 Rotate the blocks as shown in the quilt assembly diagram above right. Sew six rows of six blocks each. The quilt should now measure 60½" square.

2 Join the two yellow 5¾" x 42" border strips end to end and join the two orange 5¾" x 42" border strips end to end. Press the seam allowances open. Measure the quilt from top to bottom through the middle to determine the length of the side borders. From each pieced strip, cut a side border to the measured length; attach the yellow strip to one side of the quilt and the orange strip to the opposite side.

3 Join the two pink 7¾" x 42" border strips end to end and the two green 7¾" x 42" border strips end to end. Measure the quilt from side to side through the middle including the side borders to determine the length of the top and bottom borders. Trim each strip to the measured length; attach the pink border to the top of the quilt and the green border to the bottom.

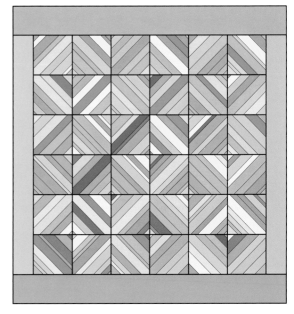

Quilt assembly

## Finishing the Quilt

Go to ShopMartingale.com/HowtoQuilt for free downloadable information on finishing your quilt.

1 Piece and trim the backing to measure approximately 6" larger than the quilt top.

2 Layer the backing, batting, and quilt top; baste. Quilt as desired.

3 Trim the excess batting and backing even with the quilt top.

4 Use the 2¼"-wide striped strips to make and attach double-fold binding.

# Glory Boxes

*What a fun use for 1930s reproduction prints—or any collection of cheerfully colored fabrics! Whether you see stars or sets of three-dimensional boxes when you look at this quilt, it's sure to please.*

## Materials

*Yardage is based on 42"-wide fabric; fat quarters are 18" x 21".*

8 fat quarters of assorted blue, green, yellow, lavender, and red prints for blocks and pieced border
4 fat quarters of assorted red prints for pieced border
1⅓ yards of white muslin for blocks, sashing, and inner border
3 yards of fabric for backing
½ yard of red print for binding
50" x 59" piece of batting

## Cutting

*All measurements include ¼"-wide seam allowances. Make all cuts across the 18" width of your fabric quarters, not the 21" length.*

From *each* of the 8 assorted fat quarters, cut:
2 strips, 3" x 18"; crosscut into 10 squares, 3" x 3" (80 total)
3 strips, 1½" x 18"; crosscut into 10 rectangles, 1½" x 4½" (80 total)
4 strips, 1½" x 18"; crosscut into 20 rectangles, 1½" x 3½" (160 total)
2 strips, 1½" x 18"; crosscut into 10 rectangles, 1½" x 2½" (80 total)

From *each* of the 4 red fat quarters, cut:
20 squares, 3" x 3" (80 total)
1 square, 4½" x 4½" (4 total)
1 rectangle, 1½" x 4½" (4 total)
1 rectangle, 2" x 4½" (4 total)

From the white muslin, cut:
5 strips, 2½" x 42"; crosscut into 80 squares, 2½" x 2½"
15 strips, 1½" x 42"; crosscut into:
    172 squares, 1½" x 1½"
    31 rectangles, 1½" x 8½"
5 strips, 1½" x 42"

From the red print for binding, cut:
6 strips, 2¼" x 42"

## Making the Blocks

You'll be making 20 blocks; each block contains four units. To make one unit you'll need one white 2½" square for the center, two white 1½" squares for corners, two rectangles of one color measuring 1½" x 2½" and 1½" x 3½", and a second pair of rectangles in another color measuring 1½" x 3½" and 1½" x 4½".

1 Join the shorter rectangles to the center square as shown. Then join the longer rectangles to the center square. Press the seam allowances outward. The units should measure 4½" x 4½".

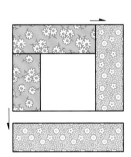

2 Draw a diagonal line on the wrong side of 160 white 1½" squares. Place the squares on the corners of the longer rectangles of the step 1 units as shown. Sew on the diagonal line, trim, flip, and press. Repeat steps 1 and 2 to make 80 of these units.

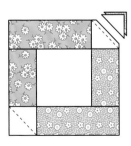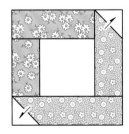

Make 80.

Pieced by Mary Ellen Thiets; designed and machine quilted by Le Ann Weaver

**Quilt size:** 45½" x 54½" • **Block size:** 8" x 8"

3 Rotate and position four units from step 2 as shown to form a block. Note that the corners of the longest rectangles are always at the center of the block. Sew the units together and press as shown. Make 20 blocks. Your blocks should measure 8½" x 8½".

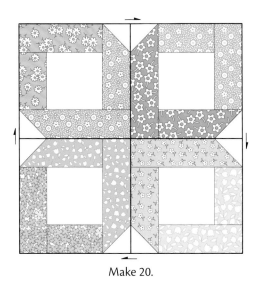

Make 20.

## Assembling the Quilt Top

1 Arrange your finished blocks on a design wall, in five rows of four blocks each, until you have a pleasing arrangement.

2 Add a white 1½" x 8½" sashing strip between each block and sew the blocks into rows.

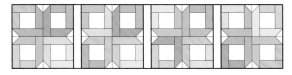

Make 5.

3 Make a horizontal sashing strip by joining four white strips, 1½" x 8½", with three white 1½" squares. (Using cornerstone squares makes it easier to line up the blocks.) Make four.

Make 4.

4 Sew the block rows and sashing rows together to make the quilt center. Press the seam allowances toward the sashing.

5 Stitch three of the five white 1½"-wide strips together end to end. Measure the quilt vertically through the center and cut two white strips to this length. Sew the strips to the sides of the quilt and press the seam allowances toward the border.

6 Measure the quilt horizontally through the center and trim the remaining two white strips to this length. Sew the strips to the top and bottom of the quilt and press the seam allowances toward the border.

7 For the pieced outer border, mark a diagonal line on the wrong side of all 80 assorted print 3" squares. Using the 80 assorted print squares and 80 red 3" squares, make 160 half-square-triangle units. Trim the units to measure 2½" square.

2½"

Make 160.

8 Join four half-square-triangle units to form a diamond unit, rotating the squares so that the red prints are on the outside corners as shown. The units should measure 4½" square. Make 40.

Make 40.

9 Join 11 diamond units to form a side border. Add a red print 2" x 4½" rectangle to each end of the border. Make two. Measure the quilt through the center in both directions, including the inner borders, and write down the measurements. Cut the side border strips to fit the vertical measurement, trimming equal amounts from each end. Sew to the sides of your quilt and press the seam allowances toward the inner border.

Make 2.

$10$ Join nine diamond units; repeat to make two for the top and bottom borders. Add a red print 1½" x 4½" rectangle to each end of the top and bottom borders. Using the horizontal measurement from step 9, cut the top and bottom borders to fit, trimming equal amounts from each end. Add the red print 4½" corner squares to the ends of the borders; sew to the quilt top.

Make 2.

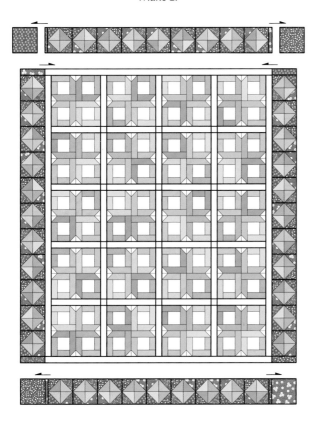

## Finishing the Quilt

Go to ShopMartingale.com/HowtoQuilt for free downloadable information on finishing your quilt.

$1$ Piece and trim the backing to measure approximately 6" larger than the quilt top.

$2$ Layer the backing, batting, and quilt top; baste. Quilt as desired.

$3$ Trim the excess batting and backing even with the quilt top.

$4$ Use the red-print 2¼"-wide strips to make and attach double-fold binding.

# Lost and Found

*Thanks to the values reversing in alternate blocks, the diagonal chain seems to appear and disappear in this super-quick quilt. The blocks are made in pairs, and each fat quarter makes two blocks.*

## Materials

*Yardage is based on 42"-wide fabric; fat quarters are 18" x 21".*

12 fat quarters of coordinating light and medium print for blocks
2⅝ yards of dark-purple print for blocks
⅝ yard of pink print for binding
3 yards of fabric for backing (crosswise seam)
54" x 78" piece of batting

## Cutting

*All measurements include ¼"-wide seam allowances.*

**From the dark-purple print, cut:**
17 strips, 3½" x 42"; from 5 of the strips, cut a total of 48 squares, 3½" x 3½"
12 strips, 2" x 42"

**From *each* fat quarter, cut:**
3 strips, 3½" x 21"; from 1 of the strips, cut 4 squares, 3½" x 3½" (48 total)
2 strips, 2" x 21" (24 total)

**From the pink print, cut:**
7 strips, 2½" x 42"

## Piecing the Blocks

Make one pair of blocks (A and B) at a time using the dark-purple fabric and one of the fat-quarter fabrics.

1 Cut a dark-purple 3½" x 42" strip in half and sew the halves to 3½"-wide strips of fat-quarter fabric. Press the seam allowances on one strip set toward the dark-purple fabric and the seam allowances on the other set toward the fat-quarter fabric.

2 Cut four 3½"-wide units from each strip set, for a total of eight units. Keep the units separated into two piles based on the direction of the seam allowances.

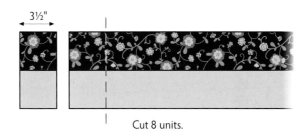

Cut 8 units.

3 Cut a 2" x 42" strip of dark-purple fabric in half and sew the halves to 2"-wide strips of fat-quarter fabric. Press the seam allowances on both strip sets toward the dark-purple fabric. Cut eight 2"-wide units from each strip set for a total of 16 units.

Cut 16 units.

4 Sew the 2"-wide units together in pairs to make four-patch units. Make eight four-patch units.

Make 8.

Pieced by Mary Green; machine quilted by Krista Moser

**Quilt size:** 48½" x 72½" • **Block size:** 12" x 12"

5 To make block A, sew four dark-purple 3½" squares, the step 2 units with the seams pressed toward the dark-purple fabric, and four of the four-patch units together in rows as shown, making sure to orient the four-patch units correctly. Press the seam allowances toward the dark-purple fabric. Join the rows. Press the seam allowances in one direction.

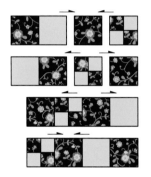 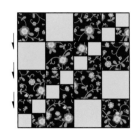

Block A

6 To make block B, sew four fat-quarter 3½" squares, the step 2 units with the seams pressed toward the fat-quarter fabric, and four of the four-patch units together in rows as shown. Again, make sure the four-patch units are oriented correctly. Press the seam allowances toward the fat-quarter fabric. Join the rows. Press the seam allowances in one direction.

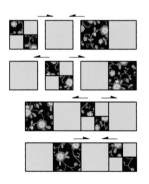 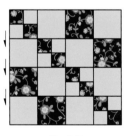

Block B

7 Repeat steps 1–6 to make a total of 24 blocks— one A and one B from each fat quarter.

## Assembling the Quilt Top

Arrange the blocks in six horizontal rows of four blocks each. Sew the blocks together in rows. Press the seam allowances in opposite directions from row to row. Join the rows. Press the seam allowances in one direction.

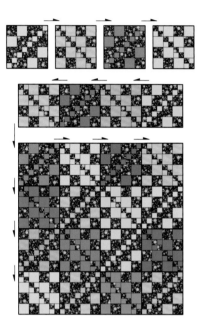

## Finishing the Quilt

Go to ShopMartingale.com/HowtoQuilt for free downloadable information on finishing your quilt.

1 Piece and trim the backing to measure approximately 6" larger than the quilt top.

2 Layer the backing, batting, and quilt top; baste. Quilt as desired.

3 Trim the excess batting and backing even with the quilt top.

4 Use the pink-print 2½"-wide strips to make and attach double-fold binding.

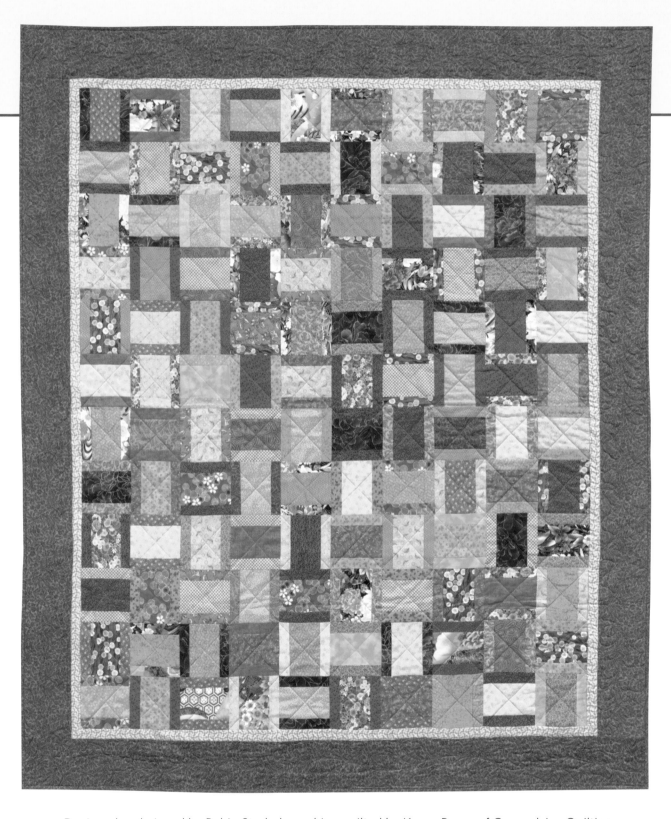

Designed and pieced by Robin Strobel; machine quilted by Karen Burns of Compulsive Quilting

**Quilt size:** 62½" x 72½" • **Block size:** 5" x 5"

# Not Manly Enough

*Choose three to five brown or tan fabrics for every turquoise (or other bright colored) one. If you like the look you get when you use a lot of different prints, use more than the minimum of 24 fat quarters.*

## Materials

*Yardage is based on 42"-wide fabric; fat quarters are 18" x 21".*

18 fat quarters of assorted tan and brown prints for blocks
6 fat quarters of assorted turquoise prints for blocks
1¾ yards of dark-turquoise print for outer border and binding
⅜ yard of tan print for inner border
3¾ yards of fabric for backing (crosswise seam)
68" x 78" piece of batting

## Cutting

*All measurements include ¼"-wide seam allowances.*

**From each of the fat quarters, cut:**
5 rectangles, 3½" x 5½" (120 total)
10 rectangles, 1½" x 5½" (240 total)*

**From the tan print, cut:**
6 strips, 1½" x 42"

**From the dark-turquoise print, cut:**
7 strips, 5½" x 42"
7 strips, 2½" x 42"

*\*Keep rectangles of the same fabric together.*

## Making the Blocks

Sew matching 1½" x 5½" rectangles to both long sides of a 3½" x 5½" contrasting rectangle. Press the seam allowances toward the darker fabric. Make 120 blocks, mixing the color combinations, but always using matching skinny rectangles in each block.

Make 120.

## Assembling the Quilt Top

1 Sew the blocks in 12 rows of 10 blocks per row, alternating the direction of each block as shown in the quilt assembly diagram on page 22. Press the seam allowances in opposite directions from row to row. Sew the rows together.

2 Piece the tan-print 1½"-wide strips end to end. From this, cut two borders, 60½" long, and sew them to the quilt sides. Cut two borders, 52½" long, and sew them to the top and bottom of the quilt. Press all seam allowances toward the borders.

3 Piece the dark-turquoise 5½"-wide strips end to end. From this strip, cut four strips, 62½" long, for the outer borders. Sew the strips to the quilt.

## Finishing the Quilt

Go to ShopMartingale.com/HowtoQuilt for free downloadable information on finishing your quilt.

1 Piece and trim the backing to measure approximately 6" larger than the quilt top.

2 Layer the backing, batting, and quilt top; baste. Quilt as desired. Trim the excess batting and backing even with the quilt top.

3 Use the dark-turquoise 2½"-wide strips to prepare and attach double-fold binding.

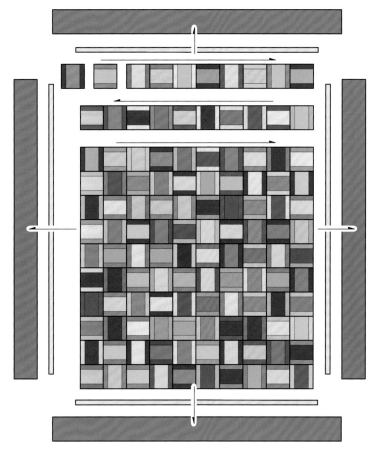

Quilt assembly

# Bright Bullion

*Nothing could be faster or easier than making this quilt! Use a dozen fat quarters and a little yardage in any color you choose, and make this bed-size quilt for a gift, a charity quilt, or even to keep for yourself.*

## Materials

*Yardage is based on 42"-wide fabric; fat quarters are 18" x 21".*

12 fat quarters of assorted prints for blocks*
2 yards of green print for sashing and inner border
1¼ yards of large-scale print for outer border
⅔ yard of blue fabric for binding
6 yards of fabric for backing
75" x 97" piece of batting

*If, after prewashing and trimming off the selvages, the fat quarters do not measure at least 18" x 21", you'll need 15 fat quarters.*

## Cutting

*All measurements include ¼"-wide seam allowances. Make all cuts across the 18" width of your fabric quarters, not the 21" length.*

From *each* fat quarter, cut:
6 strips, 3½" x 18" (72 total)

From the green print, cut:
24 strips, 2½" x 42"
8 rectangles, 1¾" x 2"
8 rectangles, 1¾" x 4½"

From the large-scale print, cut:
8 strips, 4½" x 42"
4 squares, 2" x 2"

From the blue fabric, cut:
9 strips, 2¼" x 42"

## Making the Blocks

1 Randomly sew six of the assorted 3½"-wide strips together as shown to make a strip set. Make 12 strip sets. Press the seam allowances in one direction. Cut each strip set into two 8½"-wide units, 24 total.

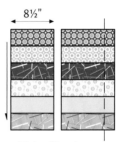

8½"

Make 12 strip sets.
Cut 24 units.

2 Using six green 2½"-wide strips, sew four units to each strip as shown. Cut apart the blocks, trimming the green strips even with the edges of the units. Press the seam allowances toward the green strip. The blocks should measure 8½" x 20½". Make 24 blocks.

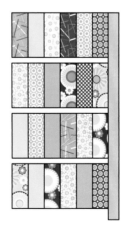 

Make 24.

Designed, pieced, and machine quilted by Le Ann Weaver

**Quilt size:** 70½" x 92½"  •  **Block size:** 8" x 20"

## Assembling the Quilt Top

1 Sew four blocks together end to end as shown to make a block row. Make six rows. Each block row should measure 8½" x 80½".

Make 6.

2 Sew 10 of the green 2½"-wide strips together in pairs, end to end, and then trim each strip to measure 80½" long. Make five sashing strips.

3 Join the block rows and the five sashing strips as shown with the sashing strips between the block rows, rotating every other row 180° as shown. The quilt center should measure 58½" x 80½".

4 For the inner border, sew the remaining green 2½"-wide strips together end to end. Cut two strips the length of the quilt for the side borders. Add the side borders, pressing the seam allowances toward the borders. Measure the width of the quilt and cut two strips for the top and bottom borders. Add the top and bottom borders and press. The quilt center should measure 62½" x 84½".

5 To make the corner blocks, sew green 1¾" x 2" rectangles to opposite sides of a large-print 2" square. Then sew green 1¾" x 4½" rectangles to

the top and bottom of the block as shown. Make four corner blocks.

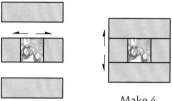

Make 4.

6 Sew the 4½"-wide large-print strips together end to end. Measure your quilt through the center in both directions and cut two side borders and two top and bottom borders to the correct measurements. Stitch the side borders to your quilt top.

7 Stitch the corner blocks to the ends of the top and bottom borders, and then sew the borders to your quilt top.

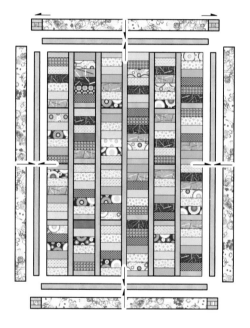

## Finishing the Quilt

Go to ShopMartingale.com/HowtoQuilt for free downloadable information on finishing your quilt.

1 Piece and trim the backing to measure approximately 6" larger than the quilt top.

2 Layer the backing, batting, and quilt top; baste. Quilt as desired.

3 Trim the excess batting and backing even with the quilt top.

4 Use the blue 2¼"-wide strips to make and attach double-fold binding.

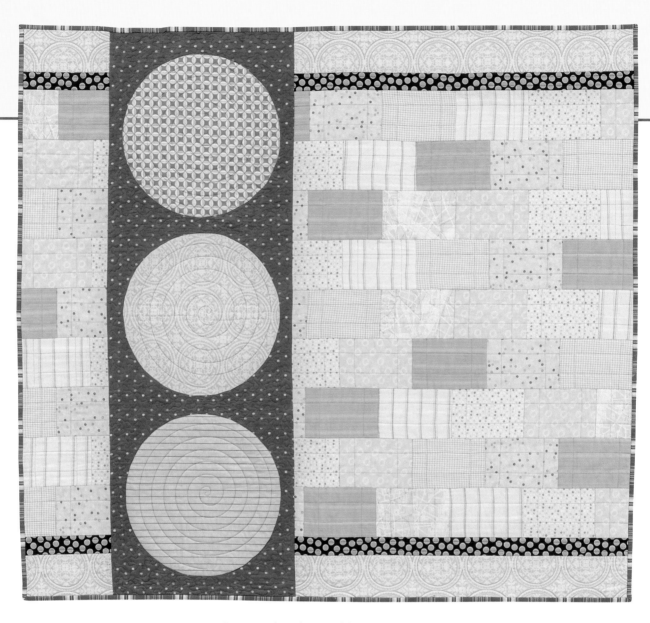

Designed and pieced by Sarah Bisel

**Quilt size:** 52½" x 48"

# Cocoa Cakewalk

*This quilt's inspiration came from the many different ways you can prepare chocolate cake—baked in the round and layered, swirled with icing, or as a sheet cake cut into generous rectangular serving pieces.*

## Materials

*Yardage is based on 42"-wide fabric; fat quarters are 18" x 21".*

1 fat quarter *each* of 7 different light prints for patchwork
1½ yards of brown print for circle background
3 fat quarters of assorted light prints for circle appliqués
⅓ yard of light-blue print for outer border
¼ yard of dark print for inner border
½ yard of striped fabric for binding
3 yards of fabric for backing
54" x 59" piece of batting

## Cutting

*All measurements include ¼"-wide seam allowances.*

From *each* of the 7 light fat quarters, cut:
8 rectangles, 4½" x 6½" (56 total; 2 will be extra)

From the dark print, cut:
2 strips, 2½" x 42"

From the light-blue print, cut:
2 strips, 4½" x 42"

From *each* of the 3 fat quarters for circles, cut:
1 circle*

From the brown print, cut on the *lengthwise* grain:
1 strip, 17" x 48½"

From the striped fabric, cut:
6 strips, 2½" x 42"

*Create a full-circle template from the quarter-circle pattern on page 29. Using the template, trace a circle on the wrong side of each of the three fat quarters. Cut out the circles, adding a ½" seam allowance all around.*

## Making the Rows

1 Arrange the 4½" x 6½" rectangles in nine horizontal rows of six rectangles each. Number the rows 1 through 9, with 1 being the top row. Join the rectangles along their short edges to make each row. Press the seam allowances of odd-numbered rows to the left; press even-numbered rows to the right.

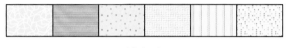

Make 9.

2 Sew each of rows 1, 3, 5, 7, and 9 into a loop, first marking the left rectangle of each row with a pin. Press the seam allowances in the same direction as the rest of the row.

Sew together.

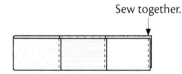

3 Cut the loop rows by cutting the marked block in half (3" from the seam line).

3"      3"

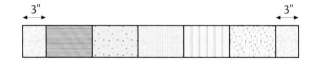

## Assembling the Quilt Top

1 Sew the nine rows together. Press the seam allowances in one direction.

2 Join a dark inner-border strip to the light-blue outer-border strip. Make two. Press the seam allowances toward the inner border.

Make 2.

3 Measure the quilt and add the border units to the top and bottom. Press the seam allowances toward the borders.

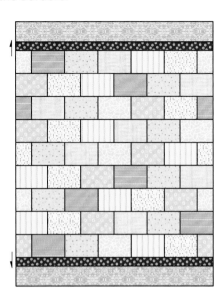

4 Cut the quilt top vertically, 7½" from the left edge.

7½"

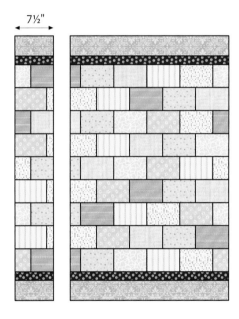

## Appliquéing the Circles

1 Find the center of the brown-print strip by folding the strip in half in both directions; finger-press to leave a crease.

2 Prepare the circles for appliqué using your favorite technique, adding a seam allowance for hand appliqué or turned-edge machine appliqué. Fold the center circle in half twice and crease well, so you can see the middle line clearly. Fold the other circles in half once and crease.

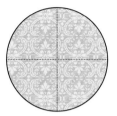

3 Pin the middle circle to the center of the background strip. Match up the middle crease in your circle with the middle crease of the background strip to ensure that your circle is centered. Pin the remaining circles in the same manner, spacing the circles 1½" from each other.

4 Appliqué the circles by hand or machine.

5 Join the circle background to the quilt top by sewing it between the smaller side piece and the larger section of the quilt top. Press the seam allowances toward the circle strip.

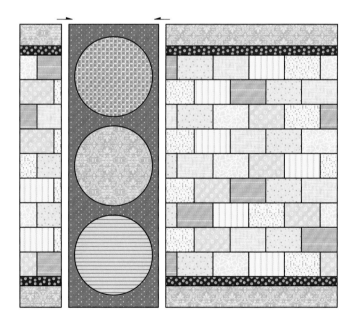

## Finishing the Quilt

Go to ShopMartingale.com/HowtoQuilt for free downloadable information on finishing your quilt.

1 Piece and trim the backing to measure approximately 6" larger than the quilt top.

2 Layer the backing, batting, and quilt top; baste. Quilt as desired.

3 Trim the excess batting and backing even with the quilt top.

4 Use the striped 2½"-wide strips to make and attach double-fold binding.

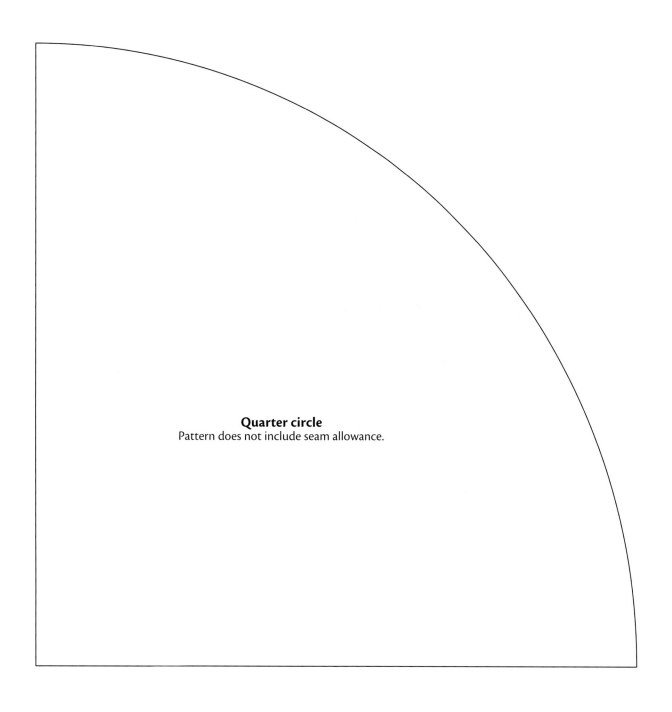

**Quarter circle**
Pattern does not include seam allowance.

Designed and pieced by Terry Martin; machine quilted by Adrienne Reynolds

**Quilt size:** 61" x 61"  •  **Block size:** 12" x 12"

# Strip-Pieced Puzzle

*The Crayon Box block works beautifully in this scrappy quilt. The blocks are all the same, but rotated to add interest and movement to the quilt design. This quilt is easy to make using strip piecing.*

## Materials

*Yardage is based on 42"-wide fabric; fat quarters are 18" x 21".*

13 assorted fat quarters for blocks and binding
1⅝ yards of multicolored print for block centers and border
4 yards of fabric for backing
67" x 67" piece of batting

## Cutting

*All measurements include ¼"-wide seam allowances. Audition the fat quarters for each of the 13 segments of the block, referring to the block diagram below. When you have determined the position of each fabric, number the fabrics with their respective position in the block.*

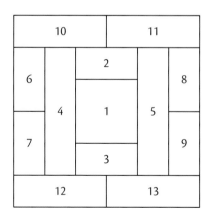

From the multicolored print (fabric 1), cut:
2 strips, 4½" x 42"; cut the strips in half crosswise to make 4 strips, 21" long
6 strips, 7" x 42"

From *each* of fabrics 2 and 3, cut:
4 strips, 2½" x 21 (cut across the longest width of the fabric (8 total)

From *each* of fabrics 4 and 5, cut:
8 strips, 2½" x 18" (cut across the shorter width of the fabric); crosscut into 16 rectangles, 2½" x 8½" (32 total)

From *each* of fabrics 6–9, cut:
2 strips, 4½" x the longest edge of the fat quarter (8 total)

From *each* of fabrics 10–13, cut:
2 strips, 6½" x the longest edge of the fat quarter (8 total)

From the remainder of the fat quarters, cut a total of:
13 strips, 2½" wide

## Making the Blocks

1 Sew a fabric 2 and a fabric 3 strip to opposite long edges of a fabric 1 strip to make strip set A. Repeat to make a total of four strip sets. Press the seam allowances toward fabrics 2 and 3. Crosscut the strip sets into 16 segments, 4½" wide.

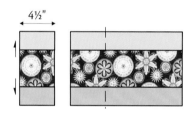

Strip set A.
Make 4. Cut 16 segments.

2 To each A segment from step 1, sew a fabric 4 rectangle to the left edge and a fabric 5 rectangle to the right edge. Press the seam allowances away from the A segments.

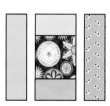

Make 16.

3 Sew fabric 6 and fabric 7 strips together in pairs along the long edges to make two of strip set B. Repeat with fabric 8 and fabric 9 strips to make two

of strip set C. Press the seam allowances in either direction. Crosscut each pair of strip sets into 16 segments, 2½" wide.

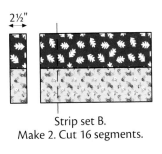

Strip set B.
Make 2. Cut 16 segments.

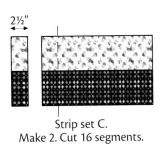

Strip set C.
Make 2. Cut 16 segments.

4 Sew a B segment to the left edge and a C segment to the right edge of each unit from step 2. Press the seam allowances away from the center.

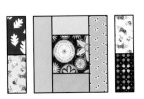
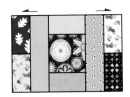

Make 16.

5 Join fabric 10 and fabric 11 strips along their long edges to make two of strip set D. Repeat for fabric 12 and fabric 13 strips to make two of strip set E. Press the seam allowances in either direction. Crosscut each pair of strip sets into 16 segments, 2½" wide.

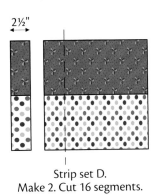

Strip set D.
Make 2. Cut 16 segments.

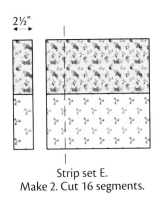

Strip set E.
Make 2. Cut 16 segments.

6 Sew a D segment to the top edge and an E segment to the bottom edge of each unit from step 4. Press the seam allowances away from the center.

Make 16.

## Assembling the Quilt Top

1 Refer to the quilt assembly diagram below to arrange the blocks into four rows of four blocks each, rotating every other block a quarter turn. Sew the blocks in each row together. Press the seam allowances in opposite directions from row to row. Sew the rows together. Press the seam allowances in one direction.

2 Sew the border to the quilt top using the multicolored 7"-wide strips.

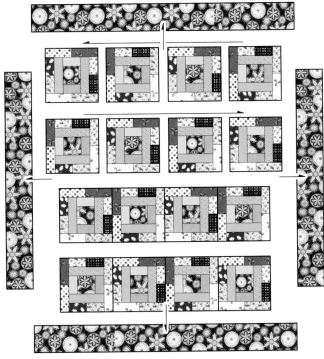

Quilt assembly

## Finishing the Quilt

Go to ShopMartingale.com/HowtoQuilt for free downloadable information on finishing your quilt.

1 Piece and trim the backing to measure approximately 6" larger than the quilt top.

2 Layer the backing, batting, and quilt top; baste. Quilt as desired.

3 Trim the excess batting and backing even with the quilt top.

4 Use the assorted 2½"-wide strips to make and attach double-fold binding.